A Complete Guide to Raising Healthy Goats

From Beginner's Basics to Expert Tips on Raising Healthy and Happy Goats for meat, milk, and fiber

ERIK MURPHY

1 | Introduction

How Owning Goats Can Be Beneficial

One of the things to research before purchasing a goat is the advantages of having one raised. The majority of farmers adore owning this mammal as cattle.

Goats are great providers of milk and meat, therefore raising them can be quite profitable. Goats can also be used to make cheese, butter, clothes, and a variety of other products, all of which can be profitable ventures.

Learning everything there is to know about rearing goats might be a simple task. As long as they have excellent guidance and are ready, anyone can begin raising goats for profit.

What makes goats so amazing? Bringing them up on your land will assist you in leading a sustainable lifestyle. Since they are among the most adaptable pets you can have.

Then why breed goats? Here are a few advantages of goat ownership.

- They Clear Land:

Live weed eaters are goats. They will remove all kinds of invasive plants, including blackberry bushes, poison ivy, weeds, and overgrown shrubs. Using goats to pull those annoying, undesired plants saves money on chemicals and lowers the possibility of forest fires. They will also consume bark, leaves, and pine needles.

Goats are picky eaters, in contrast to the common misconception that they would eat everything, even tin cans. As browsers, goats won't even consume grass unless it's their sole option. Therefore, we can assure you that having a goat will not result in a perfectly maintained lawn.

- They Produce Milk and Cheese

You can save your family money on milk by raising a dairy goat instead of having to make the long trip to the grocery store. Because they are smaller and require less land than dairy cows, they are also more economical. Are you intolerant to lactose? Goat milk is demonstrably easier to digest than cow's milk. Another application for the milk is to create a light, creamy soap.

Cheese? Please say yes. Known by its French name, chevre, this tart goat's milk cheese tastes great with toast and honey or as a tasty queso to present to guests. Alpine, Saanen, and Nubian are excellent breeds to purchase for dairy production.

- They Produce Fiber

Were you aware that some varieties of goats can yield wool? Goats that are raised for cashmere yield cashmere, while Angora and Pygora goats yield mohair. The fiber can be used to generate your yarn, which can then be used to create a range of items like blankets, sweaters, and caps. Additionally, you can sell the yarn to nearby spinning businesses. Castrated male goats and female goats are the best goats to raise for fiber.

- They Are a Great Meat Source

Goat meat also referred to as chevon, is the most popular red meat consumed worldwide and has grown in popularity in the US in recent years. The meat is a lean, nutritious source of protein that resembles venison. Compared to chicken, it has less fat and more protein. Finding chevon can be challenging unless you're rearing your own.

- They Make Manure

Farmers and gardeners can benefit greatly from using goat dung as fertilizer. Because of its high nitrogen and phosphate content, it is ideal for producing flowers or vegetables. Because the pellets are naturally dry, gathering and applying them is simple. Once dried out, the pellets have no smell, unlike cow manure. Additionally, the dung is a great source of fire fuel.

- They Make Great Companions

It's not always clear that goats are a better pet option than a typical cat or dog. What youngster asks their parents for a goat for months after returning home? Nonetheless, goats behave like dogs—they are devoted, lively, and gentle with young ones. With their parkour leaps, these adorable and humorous animals can even lift your spirits when you're feeling down. Remember that goats are herd animals; although they may form bonds with other farm animals, having one of their own will be beneficial to them.

Understanding the Basics

- Goat Breeds:

The choice of breed is frequently the first step in raising goats. Choosing from over 300 breeds could seem like a daunting undertaking. Only a small number of those breeds, nevertheless, are typical in the region you happen to be in. For instance, the Spanish meat goat, pygmy goat, Boer goat, Kiko goat, and Tennessee fainting goat are some of the most well-liked goat breeds in the US.

Heritage goats are older, more uncommon breeds of goats. These goats are usually more expensive and more difficult to find. However, a heritage breed like a Saanen, Toggenburg, Nubian, or French Alpine would be the best option if you intend to produce show-quality goats.

- They Need, Food, Water, and More

Now that you've decided on the type of goats you want to purchase, what next? The demands of your herd are the next thing you should think about. Goats require a large amount of area; the more you have, the more space they'll want. The ideal habitat combines open pastures or places with modest forest cover with protection from the elements. Since most goats don't fare well in the rain, snow, or extreme heat, it's critical to make sure they have access to a warm, secure area to hide.

Goats require food in addition to shelter. Roughly 90% of a goat's diet should be made up of hay. Domestic goats require vitamins and minerals in addition to hay. These can be obtained from grains, salt licks, specially-made goat pellets, and sometimes even fruits and vegetables. Finally, you must always have access to a clean water supply if you want to raise goats.

- Female Goats Need to be Milked

After obtaining food, water, and shelter for your goats, the next thing to think about is their care. This is particularly crucial if you intend to buy nanny goats—mothers who have children—to use their milk. Similar to cows, dairy goats require daily milking. Additionally, you'll need to decide what to do with the young goats. You can sell them, grow your herd, or butcher them for a meal.

- They Have to Be Fenced In

Although it may seem obvious, one of the most crucial parts of rearing goats is keeping them enclosed. Your goats' size and strength should correspond with the relative strength of your fencing. For instance, compared to pygmy goats, huge Boer goats—which can weigh over 300 pounds—need a far sturdier fence. Furthermore, since goats enjoy scaling objects, you'll also need to make sure they can't go over your fence.

- Goats Can Get Sick

Goats are largely disease-resistant, although they can still become unwell. Thus, if you're considering taking a herd home, think about the medical attention that will be needed. Your goats must first be vaccinated and inspected by a livestock veterinarian regularly. If you choose a goat breed with a lot of fur, such as an Angora, you will also need to determine if you will take care of the goat's fur yourself or hire a groomer.

Finally, every goat you bring home needs routine hoof care. The hooves of goats require trimming every four to eight weeks. Although most goat owners choose to handle this themselves, it can seem intimidating at first.

- They Can be Fun to Raise

Lastly, keep in mind that raising goats can be a lot of fun if you're considering doing so. Goats can be witty, curious, and even stupid at times. If you're prepared to put in the effort required to care for them, they may be a great addition to any hobby farm or farmstead.

2 | Choosing the Right Breed

On a farm, goats are usually among the most well-liked animals. It should come as no surprise given that they are capable of producing both wonderful meat and milk. If you can choose the breed that's best for you, these animals can make wonderful friends, according to many farm owners.

Selecting a goat breed to grow is a very difficult task. However, you shouldn't select your goats the same way you select pets—usually based on size, color, or look. You really should pick the breed of goat that will best assist you in achieving your objectives if you want your goats to fulfill a specific role, like dairy or meat production.

Best Goats for Meat

Goat meat may be quite tasty, despite being one of the less common kinds in North America. It can be a great addition to your daily diet because it can provide your family with nutrition without being overly greasy or high in calories. Not all goats, meanwhile, are suited for producing meat; some are better suited for dairy products, and yet others are best for just providing companionship.

Boer Goats

Among the many different types of goats on this list, Boer goats are by far the most popular breed for meat production. Their bodies can weigh up to 300 pounds, which makes them an excellent source of meat. One of the top goat breeds for meat in South Africa, this breed was first developed there.

Not to add that they are simple to breed due to their amazing fertility rate. These goats typically have different types of colors and come in a range of hues, such as black, red, brown, or white. Goat lifespans vary, although Boers can live up to 12 years old. They have a 20-year lifespan if given the right care.

Pros:
- Docile
- Disease resistant
- Ideal for hot and dry climates

- Matures in 90 days
- Boers grow up to 340 pounds in weight

Cons:

- High feed needs
- Prone to parasite infestation

Spanish Goat

Spanish goats are an excellent choice if you're looking for a low-maintenance breed because of their comparatively low requirements. This breed, which was first bred in Spain and later imported to the US through Mexico, is highly renowned for producing meat. Additionally, they maintain their breeding habits all year round. Goats that are in estrus, or when they are in heat, will remain in heat for 18 to 22 days.

The 1980s saw the rise in popularity of Spanish goats for meat, which are easily identified by their long, twisted horns. In the past, Spanish goats were the main supplier of goat meat, but Boer goats have now surpassed them.

Like many breeds, Spanish goats serve a variety of functions and are still a wonderful choice for producing meat. Spanish goats are an excellent addition to your farm if you require help managing extremely invasive brush species, such as buckthorn.

Pros:

- Produces savory meats
- Resistance to parasites and diseases
- Can be crossbred for higher meat, milk, or cashmere production
- Ideal for brush-clearing
- Breeds out-of-season

Cons:

- Does not yield a significant quantity of milk; as a purebred, it is not adaptable enough to be utilized for dairy production.
- Difficult to manage – flighty

Kiko Goats

Kiko goats' adaptability to living in less-than-ideal environments has contributed to their growing appeal. Like Boer goats, they can become huge in a short period.

Due to its capacity to produce a lot of meat, this breed was first introduced in New Zealand and then brought to the US in the 1990s. Kiko yields tasty milk and substantial meat that you can use to your benefit, unlike some other breeds.

They are also a great option for farms that include other animals, like sheep, because they help to soften the hard ground. When compared to Boer goats, several farmers discover that this breed is also among the more affordable ones.

You will discover that they favor worse-quality areas for grazing. Compared to other goat breeds, Kiko goats require a great deal less maintenance, which might make them a great option for novices.

Pros:

- Delicious meat

- Quickly adapts to poor climate

- Requires minimal maintenance

- Great for breeding

- Natural resistance to parasites

Cons:

- Difficult to manage because of their size and demeanor

Kalahari Goats

There's no denying that Kalahari goats are exceptionally stunning to look at. If you were to contrast them with some of the more conventional breeds that are meat-friendly, this would be especially true.

These South African-bred goats have a body that is perfect for handling heat, and their flesh is lean and excellent. When compared to meat from other breeds, this flesh is significantly more delicate and easy on the stomach.

Being immune to the majority of goat-related ailments makes Kalahari goats an extremely resilient and dependable breed, which is one of the reasons you should think about keeping them on your farm.

Even when breeding season is over, Kalahari are known to breed reliably. You might encounter up to three children every two years on average. Although they can be bred with heartier breeds to improve their total body size, they are generally tall and long-bodied.

Pros:
- Kids grow quickly
- Highly heat resistant
- Less susceptible to disease
- Highly adaptable and resilient

Cons:
- Hard to acquire
- Could be temperamental

Best Goats for Milk

You should think about the type of market you want to enter before searching for the best milking goats. Breeds with high-yielding milk output may be what you're looking for, or you may be more interested in high-fat content milk for making cheese.

In any scenario, breeds of dairy goats are something you should research. While technically every breed of goat will yield some milk, you should look for breeds that yield a significant amount. The greatest dairy goats will add to your farm's inventiveness and have few drawbacks, much as the best meat goats. Consider some of the following breeds of dairy goats:

Alpine Goats

Alpine goats can yield up to two liters of milk each day on average. For the typical household, that is more than sufficient, particularly if you have multiple goats on your land.

The fact that Alpine milk is good for more than just drinking will win you over. They have a 3% milk fat production capacity. This enables their milk to be used to make cheese, butter, and ice cream.

An Alpine goat has strong maternal instincts and a very adaptive nature, making it extremely herd-oriented. They might therefore be a fantastic complement to your current farm animals. Furthermore, compared to other goat breeds, they produce a significantly higher amount of milk because they are categorized as dairy breeds. They have an 8 to 12-year lifespan on average.

Pros:
- Very friendly and social
- Large dairy production; heavy milkers
- Easily adaptable to climate
- Protective of family
- Strong goats – can be used as pack animals
- Can be used for meat; good use for wethers if you don't want a lot of male goats

Cons:
- Highly protective of offspring

Nubian Goats

Some of the greatest goats for milking are Nubian goats. They were the most popular goats to keep on farms because they were first bred in England between 1920 and 1930.

Nubian variations yield milk with a significantly higher fat content than Alpine varieties, which might assist you in preparing fattier items like butter and cheese. It's also crucial to remember that this breed is incredibly fruitful and will almost certainly give birth to twins, triplets, or quadruplets even after the age of 12.

Compared to other breeds, Nubian goats don't yield as much milk per goat. They can produce up to 1.5 gallons on average. Having said that, their milk is also among the most flavorful available, which is another reason it's perfect for goat cheese.

They continuously produce milk as well. Finally, you'll recognize this breed's intelligence, which can be a valuable asset to your farm. Wethers in particular are excellent pack animals when it comes to Nubian goats. Nubian wether goats are another source of meat.

Pros:
- Incredibly fertile
- All-purpose breed
- Lives for many years, 15 – 18 years
- Fantastic pack animals

Cons:
- Very noisy
- Requires a lot of attention
- Sensitive to cold
- Minimal milk production

Toggenburg Goats

Goats of the Toggenburg breed are among the oldest that humans are aware of. The 1600s were when they were first reported to have been spotted. They are simple to identify in a crowd thanks to their recognizable appearance. Toggenburg goats have a fairly straight face, long beards, and a somewhat large body for their head size.

In contrast to some of the other breeds we have covered thus far, Toggenburg goats provide milk with a low-fat content (around 3%). Because of this, it's better to drink than to manufacture cheese or butter.

You will be grateful that these goats are likely to breed well because they do so frequently and can be counted on to produce babies periodically. Toggenburgs have a lengthier gestation time than other goat breeds when it comes to how long a pregnant goat will take. A Toggenburg goat doe's gestation duration is typically 179 days.

They are also highly resilient, which can be advantageous for producing milk and meat (particularly in the weather), according to several farm owners.

Despite being one of the most sought-after goat breeds worldwide, they are not suggested for novices. Goat handling experience is necessary for toggenburgs, especially during their pregnant years.

Pros:

- Resilient with cold temperatures
- Strong maternal instincts
- Up to 20 months of lactation
- Milk is sweet
- Dual-purpose goat for milk and meat

Cons:

- Not ideal for beginners
- Poor tempers
- Likely to break out of farms

Nigerian Dwarf Goats

For farmers with limited space, Nigerian dwarf goats are among the greatest milking goats. Usually, they reach half the size of an ordinary goat.

This breed is commonly seen on urban farms because it requires little area for grazing or raising children. This is particularly true in comparison to larger breeds of goats, including Boer goats.

Every day, this breed can yield up to two quarts of milk. You'll milk them in less time, yet still less than other goat breeds. Additionally, their milk has an exceptionally high butterfat content, making it far more delicious than the majority of other varieties.

Up to 6% of their desired, creamy milk is made with butterfat, which contributes to both its rich, creamy texture and flavor. They are therefore perfect for ice cream, cheese, and various types of butter.

Nigerian dwarf goats are great for kids because they are amiable and can grow to a maximum height of 23 inches. This makes them an excellent choice if you're short on space on your farm. They can have a lot of force behind their horns, so it's a good idea to get them removed when they're young. They can live to reach 15 years old if given the right care.

Pros:

- Family-friendly
- Easy to maintain
- Holds their value
- Incredibly delicious milk

Cons:

- Difficult to milk
- Easily escape from fencing
- Attractive to predators
- Jumps very high

Oberhasli Goats

Oberhasli is one of the greatest breeds of dairy goats to consider if you're seeking sweet milk. Their milk tastes far sweeter than others and has less than 4 percent fat. Depending on their living circumstances and size, this breed can yield up to 1.5 gallons of milk on average per day, however, ice cream is the most common application for their milk. They are an excellent companion for tiny farms with little area and urban farms, as they are yet another compact variety.

Oberhasli goats are wonderful for family-friendly settings due to their wonderful personalities, which is something you're sure to adore about them. Nevertheless, you should not undervalue this breed's strength. Because they can inflict serious harm if mistreated, most breeders will have them have their horns removed while they are young. Oberhaslis people live about 8 to 12 years.

Pros:
- Adaptable to weather changes
- Quite hardy
- Delicious and sweet milk
- Pack animals
- Efficient with feeding

Cons:
- Loud
- Easily escapes confinements

- Low butterfat content
- Variable production of milk

Best Goats for Pets

Having a variety of goat breeds on your property can be very beneficial for producing milk and meat. However, you may also be searching for a pet that will get along well with your children.

Goats make excellent family pets for farmers, while certain breeds are more suited to this role than others. What breeds of goats make the finest pets?

Choose breeds of goats with calm temperaments that are safe for all members of the family to be around while looking for the best goats for pets. A few of the most well-liked varieties of domestic goats are listed here.

Pygmy Goats

Pygmy goats are quite popular with farms looking for a smart and amiable companion, and they are regarded as some of the best milk goats in the world.

This breed's exceptional ability to adapt to most weather conditions makes them perfect for living on any continent. As implied by their name, they are far smaller than other breeds. On average, they survive for 12 years.

In actuality, Pygmy goats may grow to a maximum height of 15 inches and a maximum weight of 85 pounds. Despite their diminutive appearance, they yield a significant quantity of milk—more than plenty for a small household. You could typically get up to two quarts of milk that contained up to 11% butterfat daily.

Pros:

- Fun and interactive
- Friendly
- Small in size
- Produces plenty of milk

Cons:

- Needs constant attention
- Requires medical tests; susceptible to diseases

- Likely to escape enclosures

Mini Alpines Goats

Like their larger counterparts, Alpine goats are renowned for producing some of the greatest milk. Your kids will adore having Mini Alpines as family pets, especially if they're active.

The hyperactivity of the tiny alpine goat breed is widely known. Your whole family will likely be captivated for hours on end as they prance around their enclosure.

With a maximum height of 30 inches, they are also quite modest, but their body weight can reach up to 135 pounds.

Because this breed is perfect for any temperature, you'll discover that Pygmies and Mini Alpines have a lot in common, particularly when it comes to weather resilience. Recalling that your Mini Alpine would do almost anything for food is a terrific tip that can help with training.

Pros:

- Can be milked
- Very friendly
- High energy output

Cons:

- Likely to escape enclosures
- Can be heavy

Myotonic Goats (Mini Fainting Goats)

Mini Fainting goats, also called Mini Myotonics, have become incredibly popular on farms throughout the United States because of their innate tendency to "faint" in response to loud noises or unexpected events. Find out more about goat fainting causes.

Sadly, in the late 1980s, this breed of goat was listed as endangered. However, to preserve their population, they have now engaged in regular breeding. Depending on their food and level of exercise, Mini-Fainting goats can grow to be up to 150 pounds and 25 inches tall on average.

Fainting goats are a great addition to your farm because they are easy to care for and suitable for first-timers with a low maintenance requirement.

Myotonic goats tend to be friendlier than other kinds, so your kids will adore having the duty of caring for them. It's also crucial to remember that this Mini Fainting breed is more well-known for its ability to produce meat than milk. However, these characteristics might not be your priority as a pet.

Pros:

- Easy to contain
- Adapts to most environments
- Easily bred
- Produces tender and flavorful meat

Cons:

- Difficult to obtain
- Quite expensive
- Easy prey

Mini Lamanchas Goats

Mini Lamanchas are a famous breed of goat that is available in smaller sizes. They are particularly popular in petting farms around the United States. Compared to other varieties, they are significantly less likely to be hostile due to their calm temperaments and herd mentality.

They are therefore a fantastic addition to a setting that is family-friendly. Their ears are among their most recognizable features. In addition to their tiny stature and low weight, they are adorably little and hardly noticeable. Mini Lamanchas are available in a variety of color combinations, and when cared for properly, their short, glossy hair is well-known for its qualities.

Additionally, they yield a lot of milk relative to their size, with up to 4% of it being butterfat for flavorful spreads and cheeses.

Pros:
- Incredibly friendly
- Ideal house pets

- Very calm

Cons:
- Highly intelligent
- Likely to escape enclosures

When choosing a goat breed, take into account this list. First, determine if you would prefer an amiable family pet or a sizable yield of milk or meat. Goats come in a variety of varieties for a variety of uses, including fiber production and removing weeds and brush.

Certain varieties are incredibly adaptable, producing an abundance of meat and milk with a gentle disposition. Some are better suited for lone chores, depending on what you believe is missing from your farm.

All things considered, these are immensely beneficial animals that every farm owner should think about purchasing to revitalize their operation. Goat farming is another profitable endeavor.

3 | Building a Goat House or Shed

Your goats will feel safe and secure in a goat shelter, shielded from inclement weather and potential predators. The style of shed you choose will rely on your needs and financial constraints, but it should always give your goats a safe and cozy place to live.

Things to Consider Before Constructing Goat Housing

Goats may be rather destructive, therefore it's important to choose materials that are strong enough to survive their activity and the odd head-butt. It also requires a strong roof that shields from inclement weather and offers enough shade.

Another important consideration when building a goat shelter is ventilation. As a result of ammonia buildup from urine and feces, poor air quality can cause respiratory issues. Good ventilation helps prevent these issues.

Your goat shed should be conveniently located for feeding, cleaning, and keeping an eye on your animals' health, but it should also provide them enough solitude to slumber in peace.

Different Types of Goat Sheds

- One kind is an open-air shelter, which gives the goats lots of natural light and fresh air. But it's possible that this shed won't offer enough defense against bad weather.
- A run-in shed, also called a three-sided shed with a roof, is another style. While allowing for adequate ventilation, this shelter provides greater protection than an open-air shelter.
- Another choice is a goat house built like a barn and completely enclosed. Although it offers the best protection from the weather, additional ventilation systems could be needed to keep the airflow properly.
- If you have sheds or outbuildings already, you might think about turning them into goat houses by adding doors or windows, for example.

How to Build a Goat House/Shed

Start by selecting an appropriate location for the shed that is safe from predators and has proper drainage. It should also provide adequate ventilation and sunlight while keeping out harsh winds.

Next, decide on the type of goat shed you want to build based on your budget, materials available, and preference. You can choose from open-sided sheds or fully enclosed ones with windows or vents.

The construction material for your goat shed can vary from wood to metal, depending on what's readily available in your area. Make sure all materials used are sturdy enough to withstand extreme weather conditions.

Make sure the building is tall enough for the goats to stand comfortably on their haunches and has enough room for food troughs and sleeping quarters.

How Much Room Is Needed for Goats?

The quantity of room needed for the animals is one of the most important considerations when it comes to housing goats. For stall-fed goats, a 20 m × 10 m enclosure is considered sufficient in a commercial goat farm setting with 100 goats.

Goats are guaranteed enough room in their paddocks for exercise and wandering. Each animal should be able to roam around freely in the enclosure without feeling crowded or claustrophobic.

Why do Goats that are overcrowded or fight frequently sustain injuries that could be avoided with a well-designed paddock?

Construction Materials for Goat Sheds
The overall toughness, security, and comfort of your goat shed are greatly influenced by the building materials used in its construction. It is essential to select materials

that will survive inclement weather and protect your goats from predators.

Owing to its accessibility and low cost, wood is one of the most widely used materials for building goat huts. Hardwood or softwood might be used, depending on your budget. But, you have to make sure that the wood is treated to stop termites and rotting.

Because metal sheets withstand harsh weather conditions like severe rain or snowfall, they are also frequently used. They give enough protection from predators and have good ventilation.

One durable and lightweight material for goat shelter construction is PVC. Because they are impervious to rust and corrosion, they are perfect for humid environments where conventional metal sheets often corrode.

Concrete or brick blocks have the longest lifespan but are more expensive than other materials. Since these constructions retain cold air far more than wooden ones, it is imperative to maintain sufficient insulation during the winter months.

The durability of your goat shelter and its ability to keep your goats safe and comfortable will depend on the material choice you make during building.

Essential Features of a Good Goat Shed

- Having a well-built goat shed is crucial to the security and comfort of your goats. It should be spacious enough to hold all of your goats without becoming too crowded. Additionally, the shed needs to have good ventilation so that fresh air may flow throughout the whole enclosure.

- A well-insulated goat shelter is another essential component. This keeps your goats warm in the winter and aids in temperature regulation.

- Furthermore, it's critical to have enough lighting within the goat shed. This makes it simple for you to watch your animals and guarantees that, on cloudier days, they will have access to light if needed.

- Make sure there are no protrusions or sharp edges that could hurt your goats when designing a shelter for them. A slanted roof will allow rainwater to adequately drain away and prevent inside water damage to the shelter.

Maintenance Tips for Keeping Your Goats Safe and Comfortable in the Shed

- The health and welfare of your goats depend on you keeping their shed tidy and cozy.

- It's crucial to routinely clean the goat shed's bedding.

- In addition, you need to make sure the goat shelter has adequate ventilation. Static air can create respiratory issues, which can be avoided with adequate ventilation.

- Examining the structure for signs of wear and tear and damage is another maintenance suggestion. Inspect for any sharp edges that could endanger your goats as well as any gaps or fractures that could allow drafts during the winter.

- It's also critical to maintain clean, conveniently available food and water sources for your goats inside their shelter. Spoiled feed can result in digestive problems, while tainted or dirty water might cause disease or dehydration.

Cleaning and Maintenance of the Goat Shed

- The health and welfare of your goats depend on you maintaining a clean and well-kept goat shed. Frequent cleaning will stop the accumulation of germs, ammonia, and other dangerous materials that can cause your animals' breathing difficulties.

- You should clean your goat shed regularly—at least once a week, or more frequently if needed.

- Using a rake or shovel, remove all bedding material and manure from the walls, roof, and floor. Thoroughly clean the shed's interior using a high-pressure hose.

- After clearing the shed of all waste, it's critical to disinfect it using a solution that has been approved by veterinarians or agricultural experts. This will assist in getting rid of any germs or viruses that could sicken your goats.

- Ensuring adequate ventilation is also essential to the health of the people who live in your goat shed. Make sure there is adequate airflow by opening windows, adding exhaust fans when necessary, or both. Additionally, you can employ natural ventilation techniques, including placing vents next to ceilings along walls, to let air flow without subjecting animals to the outside.

- Use premium materials to ensure the shed can resist inclement weather during construction. To guarantee the wellbeing and health of your goats, you should also think about including necessary features such as adequate ventilation and drainage systems.

4 | Goat Fencing Requirements and Options

One of the most crucial aspects of rearing goats is having the appropriate goat fence. Selecting the proper kind of fence is crucial. This chapter will go over the needs, several options, and the reasons behind having high-quality goat fencing.

Benefits of Having a Good Fence

Establishing sturdy goat fencing has numerous advantages:

You can feel secure knowing that your goats and other guardian animals are kept inside the pen or pasture by this physical barrier.

It serves as your goats' first line of defense, whether they are tiny children or mature adults. Predators may be discouraged from entering your pasture by it. Since many predators may burrow beneath fences, squeeze through fence wires or gaps, or even jump over fences, it cannot be completely relied upon. Having said that, it still provides a minimal level of security.

It results in amiable neighbors. In addition to keeping your goats contained in their pasture or enclosure, a good goat fence keeps them off of the road, where they could cause accidents, as well as your neighbor's yard or farm field.

Fence Requirements

Although goat fence types can differ, all fencing systems should adhere to a few standard parts and requirements:

- Fence height: Standard-size goat fences should be 36-48 inches high.
- Fencing material: High tensile smooth wire, woven wire, welded wire, or other options.
- Bottom wire placement: Barbed wire should preferably be positioned a few inches above the ground as the bottom wire, and the following section of the fence should be positioned roughly six inches above the barbed wire. Predators are

deterred from digging beneath the fence by the barbed wire at the bottom, and livestock guardian dogs are prevented from excavating and escaping the fence.

- Fence posts: Spacing varies by type of post, read the fence post section for more details.
- Gates
- Electric/energizer: Optional

Goat fencing can be classified into two basic categories: temporary and permanent. We'll be concentrating on permanent fencing options for this. This kind of fence is also occasionally referred to as field fencing or perimeter fencing. Because it is more lasting, this is the greatest option for your goat farm in the long run.

If you want to use rotational grazing and will be moving your goats more regularly, a temporary fence is an excellent method to get started with fencing. On our farm, we've employed Smart Fence and electric net fencing, among other solutions.

Goat Fencing Options

There are numerous alternatives available for goat fencing. However, remember the above-mentioned fencing restrictions.

Electric Fence

The best method for keeping your goats in their yards, cages, or pastures is with an electric goat fence. For goat owners, though, it may often be frightening. You'll discover that electric fencing is a terrific solution once it's installed and your goats are educated to respect it.

There are various setup options for electric fences. These are two more typical choices:

1. High tensile wire is used in a multi-strand wire fence, with alternate wires usually being electrified. Certain wires may or may not be "hot" depending on the season, your goats' age, and the height of the pasture grass.
2. Woven wire with a hot wire strand positioned 4-6 inches above the weaved wire's top.

How does an electric fence work?

You may feel the energy "pulsing" through the "hot" or electrified wire. An animal (or goat farmer) will experience a jarring sensation when it comes into contact with the wire. Although it won't damage them, they won't find it comfortable.

The intention is for the goats to learn to stay inside the fence by connecting it to the feeling of receiving an electrical shock. For this reason, it's crucial that you correctly train your goats to stay inside an electric fence.

Cons of Electric Fence

Compared to other animals, goats require a greater physical barrier, therefore because of their larger stature, there needs to be more fences—typically electrified—and that fence needs to be closer to the ground.

In areas where the fence line is bordered by tall grass, electric fences frequently ground out and become less effective. In addition to maintaining the fence line by keeping the grass mowed, farmers must think about installing electricity directly above the fence or having a way to turn individual wires "on and off" in a multi-wire system. We also advise against utilizing an energized woven wire for the same reason.

.

High Tensile Wire or Field Wire Fence

Goat fencing frequently uses high-tensile wire. It's also applicable to electric fence systems.

When using a fence with goats, a five-strand wire fence is advised. Because it is more durable, high tensile is advantageous.

Woven Wire Fence

A fantastic choice for goat fencing is woven wire. For durability, high-tensile wire is the ideal material. Wire with a gauge of 14 is advised.

There will be variations in the woven wire opening sizes. For woven wire, a general guideline for opening spacing is 4 by 4 inches to 12 inches for vertical apertures.

Remember that smaller gaps will keep smaller animals, such as goat youngsters, inside the fence and reduce the likelihood that smaller predators may enter the pasture or pen.

Smaller apertures, however, may cause problems for young animals that have horns. Numerous yearling goats on our farm have been observed to get their heads hooked in the fence. Usually, the goats' horns will prevent them from doing this as they age.

If a goat keeps getting caught, we might temporarily place a "crown" on her head to assist teach her to stop poking her head through. This is an 8–10 inch flexible tubing that has been duct taped to the horns. The pipe will block the goat if she tries to poke her head through the fence to get food. It's a secure method of helping her break this bad behavior. A goat's vulnerability to predators or bullying by more aggressive goats may increase if it becomes entangled in a fence.

This might also indicate that it's time to relocate your goats to a new paddock so they have more pasture to graze if you're grazing them.

Welded Wire or Cattle Panels

To quickly erect a goat fence, welded wire, cattle panels, or stock panels can also be a simple choice. It can be a very costly alternative, though.

Cattle panels have been used on our property for gates and small outside pens.

Pallet Fence

Goat pallet fences may seem like a convenient and expedient way to get going. But as soon as you have the means, I implore you to upgrade your goat fencing option.

They aren't built for durability, but they can get the job done. I can recall all the times we've received delivery of farm goods and how easily the pallets can shatter. Furthermore, because pallet wood isn't treated, it will probably decay sooner rather than later.

Fence Posts

For your goat fencing, you have several alternatives for fence posts. You can occasionally utilize a mix of various fence posts.

Wooden posts: These are useful for strengthening the fence along the fence line and as corner posts, such as h-braces. For instance, the permanent fence on our farm has wooden fence posts about every 300 feet, as well as in lowing regions. T-posts will be used approximately every 16 to 20 feet, in between those spans. To ensure the longest lifespan, get treated fence posts.

Metal T-posts: When used with cattle panel fences or welded wire, t-posts are an excellent choice for shorter fence lines. They can be used with woven wire fencing or five-strand wire in conjunction with wooden fence posts, as previously mentioned.

Step in plastic posts: These are a simple temporary fencing alternative that usually uses electrified poly wire.

5 | Feeding and Nutrition

Goats are the only ruminant species that can eat and consume nearly any kind of food. Therefore, choosing what to feed goats is not a big concern if you want to launch a goat farming enterprise. You can raise goats by feeding them any kind of goat feed—natural, homemade, or made commercially.

Goat rearing is growing in popularity these days due to its many uses. Goats provide us with a variety of products, including meat, milk, hides, fiber, and more. However, effective feed supply and management techniques are largely responsible for the goat farming industry's profitable production.

A healthy diet that contains protein, energy, vitamins, and minerals is part of proper feed management. Therefore, learning how and what to feed goats is essential when beginning a goat farming business.

➢ Pasture

Making a pasture for your goats is essential, as it allows them to roam freely and consume food. Your goats will stay healthy and receive enough essential nutrients, such as protein and energy, by foraging on pasture. The goats' natural pasture diet also improves the flavor and digestion of other foods.

For the health and productivity of goats, a pasture including natural plants and grasses such as sorghum, millet, Sudan and Bahia grasses, grain grass mixture, clover, and others is highly beneficial.

Goats that are allowed to roam freely in pasture are less likely to contract numerous internal and external parasite diseases.

➤ Hay

Making a pasture for your goats is essential, as it allows them to roam freely and consume food. Your goats will stay healthy and receive enough essential nutrients, such as protein and energy, by foraging on pasture. The goats' natural pasture diet also improves the flavor and digestion of other foods. For the health and productivity of goats, a pasture including natural plants and grasses such as sorghum, millet, Sudan and Bahia grasses, grain grass mixture, clover, and others is highly beneficial.

Goats that are allowed to roam freely in pasture are less likely to contract numerous internal and external parasite diseases.

> Vitamins and minerals

Minerals and vitamins must be present in the goat diet. Because vitamins and minerals help the goats avoid many ailments and maintain their productivity. They require a lot of minerals and vitamins in their diet. Certain minerals included in the feed, such as calcium, salt, and phosphorus, are extremely beneficial to goats.

Goats greatly appreciate a premix of loose minerals, so you can supply that. Some vitamins, including vitamins A, D, and E, are also necessary for their healthy growth and production. Therefore, when feeding your goats, be sure that their regular, daily food contains all those ingredients.

You can feed your goats 12% to 16% grainy manufactured food if there isn't enough natural goat feed available where you live. You ought to provide the children with both complementary and creep food. Protein and carbons are abundant in grains. Cereal grains that are rich in energy and carbon include rye, oats, moil, corn, and barley. Goats can get enough protein from fish meal, soybean meal, cottonseed meal, and other protein supplements made from plants and animals.

> Garden and kitchen scraps

You may properly repurpose your kitchen and garden scraps by rearing goats. Scraps from the kitchen and yard are typically used by composters. However, you can feed your goats with those leftovers if you raise them. Goats will devour all those leftovers with joy.

You can give your goats a variety of common garden and kitchen waste, such as banana and orange peels, tomato and garlic skins, chopped fruit, and other veggies. Certain foods, such as fish cuts and egg shells, are not consumed by goats. Alternatively, you might feed these items to your ducks and hens.

Goats are ruminants, which means they consume nearly every kind of food that is placed in front of them. They may eat or devour papers and even show interest in them. However, since paper contains certain chemicals, feeding them any kind of paper could be harmful to their health. Goats may come across cigarettes or cigarette butts while browsing, which is also highly dangerous for their health.

Some farmers provide food for their goats, dogs, or cats. Goats and their nature are quite different from those of dogs or cats. Thus, giving your goats this kind of food could lead to major health issues. In addition to those items, nightshade, crotalaria, poke weed, peach leaves, plum leaves, and other foods are also very bad for goat health.

Additionally, fats supply energy at a rate that is more than twice that of carbs. Also referred to as lipids, fats have a crucial role in the generation of several hormones, such as steroid hormones, which are necessary for goat reproduction.

Proteins perform a variety of vital bodily tasks, including supporting muscles, controlling metabolism, and assisting children in reaching adulthood.

Small doses of vitamins are needed to maintain healthy bones and to help control a goat's metabolism.

In addition, minerals maintain the health of bones and maintain the body's oxygen supply.

For many animals, including goats, water is the most vital nutrient. Goats need between half and a full gallon of water per day, but they'll need more in the summer. Additionally, nursing caregivers should consume more water than usual.

Do Goat Feed Requirements Change as Goats Age?

Yes, without a doubt!

Newborns can survive on milk alone for a period during the early stage of life (but you should also consider creep feeding). When a child is weaned, usually at the age of two to six months, they require a high-protein diet to support their fast growth.

It should be sufficient if you have an abundance of pastures for them to graze on as they please. Try a starter/grower feed if not. These starter/grower meals are high in protein, which is what their bodies require to grow, and are gentle on the stomach.

Adult goats can still consume these diets, and grain-based meals promote faster growth.

Nutritional Disorders from Poor Feeding

Nutrient deficiencies or excesses can cause a variety of issues for goats. In addition, some plants and chemical fertilizers may be toxic to goats. Some of the most typical conditions you should be aware of are listed below.

➢ Acidosis

Acidosis in goats can be brought on by an excessive starch diet. Rumen bacteria are responsible for this disorder by converting starch to lactic acid. Acidosis manifests as despondency, stumbling, loss of food, and lack of rumination.

Goats frequently get acidosis, fast for one or two days, and then resolve the issue on their own. If not, cut back on the quantity of grains they eat.

> ➢ Enterotoxemia

Enterotoxemia can occur if your goats are fed an excessive amount of concentrated food too soon. Keep an eye out for this condition, particularly when flushing. Certain species of bacteria in a goat's small intestine may multiply too quickly and start to release lethal toxins if there is an excessive concentration.

The most prevalent sign of enterotoxemia is diarrhea, however, the condition usually ends in death quickly. Limiting the amount of concentrate you feed your goats is the major strategy to prevent this problem. Additionally, there is a vaccination available, so make sure your herd gets it.

> ➢ Bloat

As its name suggests, overeating is the cause of bloat. In particular, an excessive amount of grain or protein in a goat's diet is the reason. The animals may die from this illness in as little as sixty minutes. The main defense against this problem is to avoid giving your goats too much grain.

High-protein legumes are frequently another offender. To prevent an excessive amount of legume density in a single grazing area, make sure to mix legumes with grasses.

To ensure that goats are not very hungry when released out to graze, another tactic is to offer roughage to them beforehand. Furthermore, avoid putting them out to pasture too soon after a rainstorm or when there is still dew on the ground. Let the moisture burn off first; wet grass tends to cause foamy bloat at turn-in.

➢ Grass Tetany

Goats that consume an excessive amount of potassium in their food are usually the source of low magnesium levels, which can result in grass tetany. Wheat and rye are two types of grasses that are high in potassium.

Be sure your herd isn't grazing for an extended period to prevent grass tetany. To prevent overeating, only release your goats to pasture after you have fed them roughage. Try giving them a magnesium supplement if they already have grass tetany, which can cause convulsions, twitching of the muscles, and staggering.

> ➤ Ketosis

In the third trimester of pregnancy, nanny goats can enter ketosis. Recall that at this point, fetuses quadruple in size. And how will they not be able to consume enough food to keep their weight stable?

In such a scenario, the body starts using its fat reserves as a source of energy. Sugar is necessary for the metabolism of fat, but the doe might not have enough to keep up. Ketones can be generated, which can gradually rise to lethal amounts that cause coma and death.

This issue is more common in overweight and underweight does, which is one of the reasons it's critical to ensure your does have a body condition score of 3 before breeding.

➢ Hypocalcemia

Simply said, hypocalcemia means "low calcium." Since muscular function depends on calcium, hypocalcemia can cause symptoms including fatigue, trouble walking or even collapse.

Make sure your goats have enough supply of calcium to prevent this problem.

➢ Urinary Calculi

Goats that consume a diet high in calcium may also consume a diet high in phosphorus, which may mix with calcium to generate calculi or bladder stones. These may result in urethral obstructions, which may be fatal. The problem affects men more frequently.

Making sure your goats are getting twice as much calcium as phosphorus in their diet is the greatest strategy to prevent urinary calculi. This is known as the 2:1 ratio.

➢ White Muscle Disease

White muscle illness in goats can result from a diet low in selenium. The name "white muscle disease" comes from the damage and white streaks that the disease leaves on a goat's muscles.

Children are typically the sufferers of this illness. Inject children with vitamin E and selenium as a treatment. Selenium overdose in goats has not been well investigated, therefore proceed with caution since it may result in other, potentially fatal problems.

➢ Polioencephalomalacia

This awkward word simply means "goat polio," a disease that develops when the rumen's ability to produce thiamine (vitamin B1) is inhibited, as is frequently the case with anti-coccidiosis drugs. The most frequent cause of diarrhea in goats between the ages of three and five months is coccidiosis.

The brain is damaged by goat polio. Injections of thiamine can reverse the issue, but only if it is detected on time. Probably the ailment affects a goat that is lying on its side, head held back, legs stretched.

➢ Nitrate Poisoning

A deficiency of precipitation combined with nitrogen fertilizer may lead to grass issues in your field. Nitrogen is taken up by grasses throughout their growth, and when there is insufficient water, it converts to nitrates. Your goats may get nitrate toxicity from eating these plants, which can cause inadequate oxygen flow and ultimately result in death. Avoid applying nitrogen fertilizer to your fields during dry spells to avoid this issue.

➢ Prussic Acid Poisoning

Goats that consume leaves or branches from Prunus trees—which include cherry, plum, and peach trees—may become poisoned by prussic acid. When these plants are harmed—say, by frost—prussic acid in them transforms into hydrogen cyanide. Likewise with johnsongrass, sudangrass, and sorghum. Because hydrogen cyanide disrupts red blood cells, the body doesn't receive enough oxygen.

6 | Health and Veterinary Care

It is crucial to be aware of your goats' personalities and habits to keep an eye on their health care. Since disease symptoms are frequently subtle, any change in your pet's behavior could indicate a problem and warrant contact with your veterinarian.

However, as you gain skills, you could find that, to save time and money, you can handle some of your goat's medical difficulties without the need for a veterinarian. Any veterinarian you choose should specialize in the treatment of small ruminants, especially goats.

An animal with a unique digestive tract intended to break down materials like plants and trees is called a ruminant, similar to a goat. Your goat's breeder is a wonderful resource for finding a veterinarian with experience in caring for goats. You can also check online, ask around for recommendations, or phone nearby veterinarians to find out if they handle tiny ruminants. Just exercise utmost caution.

Numerous anecdotes exist of veterinarians who attempted an operation similar to one they would do on a dog or cat, not realizing the special needs of goat health care. The outcome was devastating, often resulting in the goat's death or lifelong harm.

Find out how many goats your prospective vet has treated in the past, as well as when the last time was, before choosing them. You should select a different veterinarian if it seems that they haven't had much expertise in providing care for goats recently. Get to know your goats so that your veterinarian can identify problems sooner in the event of an emergency. Fortunately, most goat health issues may be managed without a veterinarian's help.

For all the information you require on caring for your new goat herd at home and health care for goats, continue reading. When should you call a veterinarian instead of trying to handle something yourself? You just need to have some faith in your instincts. If you are new to goat ownership and lack experience, you should give your veterinarian a call if you have any worries about the health of your goats so they can advise you.

It's also a good idea to make some knowledgeable, helpful friends who are goat farmers in your neighborhood. With more practice, you'll be able to judge when to call a veterinarian and when it's comfortable for you to handle it yourself.

Common Goat Diseases, Symptoms and Treatment

Nobody wants their pets to become ill. However, we must prepare for the chance that they will get sick at some point in their life. If you are a goat owner, you must have some knowledge about the frequent diseases and other health issues that affect goats more than others. Here's a summary of some of the more common goat health care problems:

1. CAE in Goats (Caprine Arthritis Encephalitis)
Caprine Arthritis Arthritis is a common symptom of the infectious viral illness encephalitis. It can wipe out an

entire herd of goats and has no known cure. Adult goats can contract it from each other by coming into contact with bodily fluids like blood or excrement. There are multiple types of CAE and the symptoms depend on which type it is:

- ➤ Arthritic CAE (stiff, difficulty getting up or walking, weight loss)
- ➤ Encephalitic CAE (lack of coordination, paralysis, blindness, seizures)
- ➤ Pneumonic CAE (chronic cough, difficult breathing, weight loss)
- ➤ Mastitic CAE (hard/swollen udder, decreased milk)

Milk consumption is the most common way for it to pass from mother (doe or "dam") to offspring (kid"). Moreover, it can be transferred from adult to adult by bodily fluids like excrement.

The health care of your goat is seriously threatened by CAE. Similar to AIDS in people, it is an illness that attacks the immune system of goats. Although treating the bacterial form is challenging, goats may receive antibiotics and pain relief.

To shield their herd from illnesses like this, the majority of goat owners take extreme measures. A new goat should never be accepted until it has undergone a disease test. Don't forget to test your entire herd annually. As part of your program for caring for your goats, practice appropriate biosecurity.

The amount of persons who are permitted access to the region where you keep your goats should be restricted. This is especially important for those who may be visiting from another farm and may unintentionally bring toxins with them on their shoes or clothing. We need agricultural workers to change into specific boots that we own when they are hired.

Additionally, make sure the space your goats occupy is as tidy as possible. Ensure that their food and water are fresh and clean, free of dirt and other foreign objects.

Any new goat you bring home should be kept apart from the rest of your herd for a while before being reintroduced so you can watch for any signs. Call your veterinarian right away and keep your goat apart from the rest of the herd if you think it may have CAE.

2. CL in Goats (Caseous Lymphadenitis)

This chronic, communicable goat sickness is brought on by a bacterium. It's also known as "abscesses" at times. Your goats may experience enlargement of the lymph nodes and abscesses on their bodies that occasionally leak thick, green pus as symptoms of CL. CL can be transferred by direct contact with pus-filled wounds, by using brushes and clippers, and by touching any object in the barnyard that may have come into contact with pus, including structures, feed, equipment, and fences.

As part of your regimen for caring for your goats, segregate any goats exhibiting symptoms and get them examined by a veterinarian. Have every goat in your herd tested if a goat is diagnosed with CL, and isolate any goats that test positive to prevent the disease from spreading. The therapy for the infected animals is to have the abscesses lanced and flushed with disinfectants by your veterinarian.

Additionally, you need to exercise extreme caution because even a little touch with an infected goat can spread the disease to other goats. It's normally advised to simply cull (remove permanently) any goat with CL from your herd due to the risk and severity of the condition. Preventing CL is the simplest approach to handling it. Adopt the biosecurity and good health care practices that I previously advised for goats.

3. Johne's Disease in Goats (Paratuberculosis)
Johne's is a communicable gastrointestinal illness that can be fatal. It is primarily disseminated by contaminated manure, but it can also be transferred from an adult to a child by tainted feed, milk, or water. The fact that this sickness takes months to manifest and that a goat may be spreading the organism through its excrement before you notice it to the rest of your herd is a major concern.

It is difficult to identify and frequently goes unnoticed until a post-mortem necropsy is conducted. One of the symptoms is persistent weight loss even with a healthy appetite.

Since there is currently no approved immunization and no treatment, prevention is the key to managing this illness. Put into practice a sound goat health care plan. Maintain a "closed" herd and only purchase animals from other herds that have undergone testing. Examine the dam of any young goats you purchase from other herds. Avoid lending animals to others and keep your goats away from other animals that can harbor Johne's.

4. Coccidia in Goats

Microscopic protozoa parasitic on humans cause coccidiosis. In young goats (between two weeks and six months of age), diarrhea is typically caused by coccidia, a prevalent condition in goat health care. It's commonly referred to as "cocci" by goat owners.

Particularly when a newborn goat is weaned from its mother and when the goats are kept in small spaces where bedding, food, and water can readily become contaminated with excrement, coccidiosis occurs.

Because the typical goat resistance is still developing in small youngsters, the stress of weaning tends to impair it, which makes coccidiosis more likely to occur.

When present in tiny quantities, coccidia are generally not a serious health concern for adult goats as most of them already have some in their digestive tracts. Even if they might not have "diseased" status, they might nevertheless be "infected" with it.

Adult goats can excrete coccidia eggs, or oocytes, which can then contaminate food and water, readily infecting younger goats. Again, unless the coccidia multiplies, it's usually not a serious health issue for goats. That's when symptoms such as diarrhea become apparent.

Coccidia can cause weight gain as well as a decrease in eating. You will see diarrhea as it worsens, maybe with blood and mucus in it. Your goat will grow dehydrated and feeble. If coccidia is not identified and treated right away, it can develop into a significant health issue for goats. In as little as 24 hours, it can even cause a newborn goat to die.

Furthermore, even after a successful course of treatment, a goat may experience long-term consequences from the coccidia infection, such as restricted growth due to impaired absorption of nutrients. I realize that everything sounds awful.

Nonetheless, coccidia is a common disease among goat producers, especially in young goats. As long as you identify it and take prompt action, your goat should be alright. We've treated several of our goats that had coccidia, and they never experienced any more issues.

Many goat keepers utilize "medicated" diets as a preventative measure. They therefore have a "coccidiostat" in them. Moreover, you can mix Corid into your goats' drinking water or give them a dose of the medication orally. You can use Corid to treat your goats if they have coccidia. It is also possible to administer some sulfa medications, such as Albon and Sulmet, to stop the development of further secondary infections.

Nonetheless, coccidia is a common disease among goat producers, especially in young goats. As long as you identify it and take prompt action, your goat should be alright. We've treated several of our goats that had coccidia, and they never experienced any more issues.

Many goat keepers utilize "medicated" diets as a preventative measure. They therefore have a "coccidiostat" in them. Moreover, you can mix Corid into your goats' drinking water or give them a dose of the medication orally. You can use Corid to treat your goats if they have coccidia. It is also possible to administer some sulfa medications, such as Albon and Sulmet, to stop the development of further secondary infections.

5. Brucellosis in Goats

Although it is uncommon, brucellosis is a disease that can affect goats in the United States. Abortions of retained placenta in does, and testicular enlargement in bucks are among the symptoms.

Blood, urine, milk, or semen can all contain brucellosis, which is spread via contact with an infected animal's placenta, fetus, secretions, or vaginal discharge.

For several months, the organism can live in water, hay, dung, equipment, and clothing. There isn't a workable, effective brucellosis treatment. Maintaining cleanliness, avoiding contact with anything known to spread the disease, keeping an eye out for signs, and isolating affected animals are the greatest preventative measures you can take for your goat's health.

6. Sore Mouth in Goats

Goats frequently contract the viral illness known as sore mouth. Animals can contract it from one another through bedding and milking supplies, for example. Scabby, painful, and thick sores on the lips and gums are the symptoms. A nursing child may potentially transmit it to the dam, resulting in mastitis and sores on her udder.

In moderate situations, the illness could clear itself without the need for medical intervention; a goat's healing timeframe is one to four weeks. More serious situations might benefit from softening ointments. A serious case could be fatal for a very young child.

There are vaccines available to stop mouth sores. To offer your goats immunity for around a year, using the vaccination involves introducing a small amount of the disease into your herd. To prevent an epidemic of the disease during show season, several goat keepers have vaccinated their herd as part of their routine care for goats. However, the vaccine can result in a few minor scabs, so it's normally best to have the shot approximately six weeks before a performance so the scabs have time to heal.

I found out that a well-known goat breeder had to pull a prize-winning goat from auction due to a sore mouth outbreak in their herd, which cost them thousands of dollars. Thus, in this particular instance, immunization against sore mouth likely would have avoided a great deal of problems.

7. Toxoplasmosis in Goats

Although it is more frequent in sheep, the single-cell protozoan Toxoplasma (Toxoplasma gondii) can infect goats as well. Your goats may come into contact with this organism through eating grass or other meals infected with cat excrement, as cats are carriers of it. Cats can contract the organism by consuming placentas, raw meat, or tiny rodents.

Your goat's small intestine becomes infected, and the illness then travels through the blood to the reproductive system. Toxoplasmosis can cause weak children, mummification, miscarriage, and stillbirth.

Pregnant women are particularly at risk for contracting this disease, which can also spread to adults. As part of your routine for taking care of your goat, make sure you use gloves whenever you handle any contaminated material or animal. As of right now, there is no recognized, efficient treatment.

To prevent contracting this illness, a vaccination is available. Adhering to proper hygiene and management procedures in your goat's medical care is the second greatest defense against toxoplasmosis. Keep your goats away from cat poop.

Goat feed should be kept refrigerated and out of the reach of contamination. Don't let weird cats on your land. Placentas and fetuses should be disposed of securely so that cats cannot consume them.

8. Pinkeye in Goats

A bacterial or viral infection is the source of pinkeye, which is an inflammation of the eyelid. Because of its high contagiousness, outbreaks frequently happen when new goats are added to the herd.

Some people assert that while treatment may be necessary in extreme circumstances, the majority of cases will resolve on their own.

On the other hand, pinkeye if untreated can be fatal and cause blindness. It is therefore preferable to address it now. The most popular therapy for pinkeye is to point the affected eye two to four times a day with an antibiotic called terramycin.

9. Mastitis in Goats

The most common cause of mastitis, which is an inflammation of the mammary gland (udder), is dairy goats. It can be brought on by bacteria, viruses, or fungi and has an impact on the milk they produce. Injuries, high-stress workplaces, and poor hygiene habits can occasionally cause it. Hence, maintaining cleanliness in your goat's medical regimen is crucial.

There are two kinds of mastitis: systemic and chronic. When it comes to the systemic type, symptoms can include a raised pulse and high fever. Reduced milk supply or changes in the flavor, color, texture, or smell of the milk—which can turn yellow and runny—are common symptoms.

In addition, the udder may become painful to the touch, hot, swollen, hard, and crimson. Goats that are afflicted ought to be kept apart to prevent the spread of illness, and antibiotics should be administered if required.

To find out precisely what kind of bacteria or virus may be present, your veterinarian can test the doe's milk and/or blood. This will help you decide which drugs are best to use.

Sometimes the best course of action is to assist the goat in drying out its udder, but this takes time. To decrease milk output, this initially entails lowering the amount of grain and alfalfa in the doe's diet. To release pressure in the doe's udder, milk her gently. You can use an udder-soothing lotion such as Bag Balm during the process. To eradicate any bacteria that might be on the teats, use an antiseptic teat dip.

Maintaining clean, stress-free, and disease-free goats can help prevent mastitis. You should also keep the areas where you milk and care for your goats spotless. Use teat dips and sprays before milking, wash your hands before and after, and make sure all of your milking supplies are clean. You should also wash your goats' udders frequently.

How to Prevent Goat Diseases and Health Problems

- Physical Examination in Goat Health Care

Examining your goats regularly is one of the best preventive measures you can take to keep health issues at bay. The simplest thing to do is to keep a close eye on them while you feed and care for your goats as usual.

You must carry out this everyday task as it will teach you about your goat's typical activities. This will enable you to identify instances in which habits shift and something doesn't feel quite right.

Illnesses can take many different forms and occasionally be quite challenging to diagnose. Observe the actions of your herd and search for typical signs like exhaustion, trouble standing, limb preference, mucous discharge, and anorexia.

One of the first things you should do if you see that something is off with your goats is to take their temperature.

Whatever the issue, you can rapidly rule out some options and focus on others with the aid of this easy step.

Taking regular stock of your herd should be part of your goat health care routine.

How to Take a Goat's Temperature

Make sure you periodically take your goat's temperature, particularly if you detect something that "just doesn't seem right". While a goat's body temperature can vary based on its environment, a reading between 101.5 and 103.5 degrees Fahrenheit is thought to be normal, therefore that's what you should observe on your thermometer. Normal temperatures can change based on the season, time of day, and other environmental factors.

It is advised that you take your own goats' temperature multiple times when you are certain they are healthy as part of your routine goat health care. Take their temperature throughout the day and in various seasons. Before long, you'll be able to determine what "normal" temperatures are for your herd.

When a goat exhibits strange behavior and you take its temperature and it is one or more degrees higher than usual, you may be certain that there is a problem. An infection could be present if the fever is higher than usual. Below average, and your goat might either have an extremely serious sickness or have spent too much time outside in the bitter weather.

Generally speaking, you should always take your goats' temperature before taking any further action if you suspect any problems. You can identify potential problems with your goat more immediately if you use the temperature reading. This is serious if the temperature of your goat is too low.

Prioritize fixing this before doing anything else. In the winter, low temperatures are common, especially in young goats and sick or elderly goats. As long as they have a shed or barn where they can bundle up in some hay to stay warm, most other goats can maintain a consistent body temperature, even at quite high conditions.

It's better to avoid using a heater near goats because they can be hazardous in any case due to fire hazards. Occasionally, the focus of goat health care is on avoidance. You should not feed your goat until the temperature returns to normal if it is too low.

When a goat's body temperature is low, its digestive system won't function correctly, and feeding them during this period will only make matters worse. A goat's body can be quickly brought to a temperature of approximately 104 degrees by wrapping it in plastic and submerging it in a bathtub of water, with its head left out for breathing, of course.

To maintain the tub's temperature at 104 degrees, keep adding hot water as the water cools. Continue taking temperature readings with a thermometer until the goat's body temperature returns to normal. The ideal alternative, if the bathtub approach is unavailable, is to erect a tent around the goat using bath towels, blankets, and other materials.

Some people use their bathrooms or laundry rooms for this purpose. Next, warm the goat by using a hair dryer to preheat the air within the tent. While not as quick as the bathtub method, this is still a viable choice.

Continue until the goat's body temperature reaches a normal level after taking a thermometer reading. It is imperative to regularly practice and be prepared to take temps as part of a comprehensive goat health care program.

Goat Vaccinations

The first line of defense in goat health care is vaccination. Vaccinations increase your goats' chances of survival if they become unwell, but they cannot ensure that they won't ever get sick. The following are the most typical vaccinations your goat requires:

- CDT Vaccine for Goats

Tetanus and Clostridium perfringens types C and D immunizations shield your goats from bacterial infections and tetanus.

- Rabies Vaccine for Goats

You might want to vaccinate your goats against rabies if the disease is common in your area. Otherwise, few people regularly vaccinate their goats against rabies.

- Pneumonia Vaccine for Goats

Goats struggle to stay warm, especially in windy or damp conditions. This suggests that kids could get pneumonia quickly, hence vaccination is advised.

- Chlamydia Vaccine for Goats

The most common cause of abortion in goats is chlamydia. Vaccinating your goats against this will reduce the likelihood of problems for them during pregnancy.

Giving Injections to Goats

Be at ease—vaccinating your goats at home is not too difficult. Since they are all injection forms, administration is made simple. The time and money spent on your goat's medical care can be decreased by learning how to administer shots on your own.

With goat medications, you typically provide two kinds of injections: intramuscular (IM) and subcutaneous (SQ), which go into the muscle. IV (intravenous) injections are not typically given to you. The sort of injection required for your vaccine will be specified in the manufacturer's instructions, which you should read and adhere to.

Move your goat away from the group and ask a companion to keep it motionless. Prioritize safety by grabbing your syringe and sterile needle. You must squeeze the skin into a tent-like shape and place the needle just beneath the skin to administer an SQ (subcutaneous), or under-the-skin, immunization.

Give the injection into a pre-selected muscle after inserting the needle for an intramuscular (IM) immunization. To evenly distribute the injection, be sure to massage the affected muscle. Say "thank you" to yourself for practicing good preventative healthcare and throw away the syringe and needle. When a goat becomes infected, injections are also occasionally required to administer antibiotics.

Periodic Goat Blood Testing for Diseases

Every year, you should give your goats blood tests to ensure they are free of various diseases. You can take the blood yourself at home and have it checked by a lab. This is good goat healthcare practice. Every year, practically all goat farmers test their blood.

You will always be asked if you have had your herd tested if you ever transact with other goat farms, whether it be to purchase or sell goats. You can prepare for the test and get supplies with a fast google search. After that, you'll be prepared to undertake routine blood tests as part of your program for caring for your goat's health.

How to Draw a Blood Sample from a Goat

First and foremost, safety! Start by using a freshly sterile needle right out of the packaging to take your goat's blood. When testing blood, never reuse syringes or needles.

Next, find the jugular vein on the left side of your goat's neck. Shave the area to make it more visible if you are unable to locate it. Insert the needle after marking the entry with a marker.

At an angle that is nearly parallel to the vein itself, you want to force it up into the vein. Plunge the plunger back slowly until you see blood filling the syringe. When it fills to three ccs, stop. After taking out the needle, apply pressure for 30 seconds on your goat's neck.

The process is complete once you transfer the blood from the plunger into the test tube that was included with the items you ordered. Simple as 1-2-3! Don't give up if it seems a little awkward at first. With practice, it will get easier over time. Long-term savings of both money and time compared to needing to visit the veterinarian will make the expense worthwhile.

7 | Breeding and Reproduction

As you learn about goat breeding, it's important to first learn some of the basic terms that goat keepers use.

- Doe - A female goat
- Buck - A male goat
- Doeling - Female goat less than a year old
- Buckling - Male goat less than a year old
- Kids - Baby goats
- Wether - A castrated male goat

Additionally, a male goat may be referred to as "Billy" and a female as "Nanny" by people. Although they are accepted, the terms are regarded as slang. The terms "Buck" and "Doe" are regarded as technically correct. Additionally, you should familiarize yourself with terms about goat breeding.

- Estrous Cycle - The multi-stage reproductive cycle of a mammal
- Estrus - One stage of the estrous cycle, during which ovulation occurs

- Rut- Goats mate throughout the mating season; a buck who is "in rut" has an increase in testosterone and heightened interest in females.
- • Freshening: A doe is described as a "First Freshener" or "FF" the first time she passes her fertility test, begins lactation, and produces milk.

Goat Breeding Style

The majority of goats breed readily when paired together. Usually, it's easier to stop them from breeding than to encourage them to do so. It takes a lot more does than bucks to successfully breed goats.

A lot of goat breeders might just own one buck that produces dozens of does. It makes sense when you consider it. For the buck, breeding only takes a few seconds. However, it only takes a few seconds for the doe to mate; after that, she must endure several months of pregnancy, childbirth, nursing, and childrearing. Understandably, it requires several more attempts to complete the task.

A few herders aren't even buck owners. Occasionally, they will lease or borrow a buck from someone else to use him as a "stud buck" in breeding operations before giving him back to his original owner. Alternatively, a doe may be transferred to be bred on someone else's property and then brought back.

Please exercise caution and ensure that you obtain documentation proving that any other goats who came into touch with your goats were vaccinated against the disease before doing so.

Driveway Breeding

To allow their buck and doe to meet, breed, and then depart a short while later, two herd owners will frequently even agree to meet somewhere (such as in a driveway). This is referred to as "driveway breeding" by some.

Hand Breeding

Holding the doe in their hands to let the buck mount her is referred known as "hand breeding" by some people.

Planning the Timing of Your Kiddings

When your goat kidnaps, you should schedule it so that you can be there to assist and that it won't happen at a bad time, like in the dead of winter. Establish the optimal kidding time that you want to strive for when deciding when to breed goats. Once you get the gestation period, which is 145–155 days, count backward on the calendar to determine the estimated target breeding date.

The gestation duration may be closer to 145 days for miniature breeds like Pygmy or Nigerian Dwarf, and 150 days for other types. Of fact, that is an estimate, and we have frequently had children born many days early or, in other instances, much later. It is best to schedule the goat breeding so that there aren't too many babies born at the same time. We had about ten babies born in the week prior, and we had several restless nights in a row assisting our does in quickly delivering each of them.

Having to bottle feed, wean, and take care of so many children in a short amount of time makes it even more difficult. Controlling your goat breeding might be a better idea if you want to space out the expected kiddings at various intervals. Naturally, that is a matter of personal preference. To put it over with, you might want to have all of your children born at once. Just make sure there are additional people there to assist.

Kidding in Extreme Weather Conditions

Plan your goat breeding such that there are no babies born during periods of extremely high or low temperatures. Nigerian dwarf goats, who can reproduce year-round, are a prime example of this. Back when we lived in Virginia, we had a few Nigerian Dwarf offspring born during winter snowstorms before we turned our attention to organized goat breeding. This makes it particularly challenging to assist with the birth of new children while dealing with snow, extremely low temperatures, frozen water buckets, etc.

Additionally, it makes sense to target the colder months as opposed to the hotter ones. Children born in warmer months experience lower levels of growth and more health issues. Furthermore, we've observed that, in contrast to cooler months, our does don't appear to produce as much milk during the warmer months.

Inbreeding

Mating between members of the same immediate family, such as brothers and sisters, is known as inbreeding. This may result in genetic issues, malformations, and even death. Nevertheless, some goat farms employ inbreeding to try to highlight specific desired genetic features in their goats or to save money on purchasing goats that are not part of their own goat families. In any case, it's not recommended and ought to be shunned.

However, "line breeding" is typically accepted as acceptable. This is the mating of goats who are not linked by blood, but who may be slightly related. This is advantageous, and some goat herders use it to highlight particular traits that they find appealing in their goats. Just be cautious—it will also draw attention to negative traits.

Thus, use only premium bucks with few or no negative traits for line breeding. Goat farmers have an old joking saying that goes, "It's called line breeding if it works, and it's called inbreeding if it doesn't." This is because line breeding is usually accepted and farms that utilize inbreeding tend to keep it secret (especially when things go wrong).

When Can a Goat Start Breeding?

Take care not to breed your goats too early in life. Why? Because until a doe achieves a particular body weight, often between 60 and 70 percent of an adult doe's typical body weight, her body isn't ready to expand and safely give birth to a child. A doe maybe 4 to 12 months old when she reaches puberty and is ready to conceive. Her body isn't ready for the procedure, despite that.

A doe's body will lose nourishment when she gives birth. It could be fatal for her if she's unprepared for that. Her birth canal and uterus might not be big enough for her to give delivery. Last but not least, if a doe mate before she reaches her maximum growth potential, her growth can be stunted.

Furthermore, do not believe that leaving a young buckling with your doe would prevent her from becoming pregnant. As young as seven weeks old, a buckling can begin to procreate. The outcomes could be devastating if you're not careful. Because the pregnant doe was bred too young and her body was not developed enough to bring the kids to term and birth them, many goat keepers have seen the death of a pregnant doe during kidding.

If you are breeding a standard-sized breed doe, make sure she has reached that weight by the end of the breeding season so she will be ready. A doe of that breed should weigh at least 80 lbs or so before breeding safely.

Before allowing a doe to breed, she should weigh at least 60–70% of an adult Nigerian dwarf goat, which can reach an average of 60–70 pounds over its lifetime. Approximately eight months is when a doe can often attain the safe breeding weight for goats.

Still, a lot of breeders who wish to exercise extra caution will hold off until the doe is a year old or older. To be safe, it is advised to wait until the second breeding season to begin a doe's first litter so that by then she would have had time to attain her full adult development potential.

Age to Stop Breeding

Retaining a doe for breeding after she reaches a specific age or physical condition is the most humane approach. Unlike a human woman going through menopause, a doe does not spontaneously cease ovulating at a specific age. A doe can get pregnant at any time during her lifetime since she ovulates continuously.

All the same, giving birth to an older doe increases her risk of death and is difficult for her. Furthermore, it has been discovered that retiring your doe after she reaches the age of ten can extend her life to twenty years or more. If not, the average lifespan is only around 12 years.

Your doe will need to be kept away from bucks for the remainder of her life if you decide to "retire" her at some point. This is because a doe will always go through heat. Act morally and humanely. Retire when the time is right. They deserve to live out the rest of their days in peace and without having to go through the ordeal of giving birth every year because they will have served you well.

How to tell if your goat is pregnant

You can determine if your doe is pregnant in several ways. Some can be trusted more than others. Some require more money and work than others.

Natural Signs of Pregnancy

Examining the regular indicators is one technique to determine whether your goat is pregnant. The following are some common indicators that your doe might be pregnant:

- Missed heat cycle
- Puffy vulva
- The goat appears wider than normal
- Movement felt on the goat's right side (movement on the left side is the rumen)
- Udder starts developing (often about a month before kidding)

The issue with those tests is that their reliability is somewhat low. There are more effective methods for detecting pregnancy.

Blood Test

There is also a blood test for goat pregnancy detection. To check for pregnancy, all you need to do is send a sample of your doe's blood to a lab. A veterinarian can take the blood for you. Alternatively, you can easily save time and money by drawing the blood yourself if you have someone show you how to do it the first time.

Milk Test

You can use the milk from a doe you have that is currently producing offspring to test for pregnancy if you suspect she may be pregnant again. You can find out if your doe is pregnant again by sending a sample of milk to a lab that performs this type of testing.

Urine Test

Many individuals have inquired about using a human pregnancy test kit from a pharmacy or if a urine test can be used to identify goat pregnancy. "No" is the response. Goat hormones differ from those detected by human pregnancy tests, so a human pregnancy test will not be effective on a goat.

Goat Ultrasound

One of the most accurate ways to determine whether a goat is pregnant is using an ultrasound. However, because a qualified veterinary technician typically performs it, the cost is typically higher. Investing in the necessary tools and expertise to perform goat pregnancy tests on your own is an option if you intend to perform a lot of them.

However, that may cost thousands of dollars. One wonderful thing about ultrasounds is that they can occasionally tell how many babies will be delivered. When your doe has one or two young, it's usually more accurate. With more children, however, it becomes more difficult to pinpoint precisely.

Whatever approach you take to find out if your doe is pregnant or not, the most essential thing is to educate yourself as much as possible.

You can help the new child or kids safely join the world around kidding time if you are diligent in documenting the approximate date the doe was bred.

8 | Milking and Dairy Production

While cow's milk is the traditional "drinking milk," some consumers prefer goat's milk, which has its specialized market. It is safer for certain people to eat, and it is easier to digest for those who have dairy sensitivity.

Goats are resilient and simple to care for pets. They are cheap to keep and do a good job of foraging on pasture that isn't the best for cattle. As they are smaller than cows, they are also easier to handle. They're also pleasant, highly clever farm animals that make good companions.

Additionally, they are curious and agile, which may provide for both challenging times and enjoyable goat watching (you will need an adequate fence).

Choosing a Dairy Goat Breed

Studying the various common dairy goat breeds is the first step towards producing milk from your goats. Just a small number of the hundreds of goat breeds are frequently utilized as dairy goats.

The Swiss highlands gave rise to the Alpine, Saanen, Oberhasli, and Toggenburg varieties, all of which are highly tolerant to colder weather and less-than-ideal growing circumstances. Given their more tropical ancestry, Nubian goats thrive in hot summer climates.

Housing and Fencing Dairy Goats

A dry, clean, and draft-free environment is necessary for dairy goats. You will require a warm, enclosed barn if you plan to joke around during the winter. Enough feed is essential for a happy, healthy herd of goats. Additionally, you must ensure that your goats are fenced in a very strong manner—possibly with electric reinforcement.

How to Feed Dairy Goats

Good feed, which consists of grasses, shrubs, and woodlands for them to graze freely, is the basis that goats thrive on. It's also customary to free-feed premium hay during periods when fresh forage is scarce. Hay serves as your go-to feed during these periods. Make sure you understand the specifics of feeding goats correctly since there are a few strategies and ideas for keeping them well-fed.

Ensure that there are no plants in your goat forage area that could be harmful to your goats. To find out if you have any of them on your property, contact your county extension agent.

How to Keep Dairy Goats Healthy

Keeping your herd healthy and disease-free is part of managing them. When it comes to goats, the proverb "An ounce of prevention is worth a pound of cure" is accurate. Maintaining their health is far simpler than treating them when they become unwell. Discover the fundamentals, what to watch for, and when to visit a veterinarian when they're ill.

Establish a rapport with a nearby livestock veterinarian who specializes in goat care. The immunizations that are necessary regularly will depend on your region and the local prevalence of specific diseases. The CDT or CD&T vaccination, which protects against tetanus and

Clostridium perfringens types C and D, is a frequently administered vaccination regimen for goats.

To achieve the optimum level of protection from vaccinations, it is crucial to get vaccinated at the appropriate period (both during the year and pregnancy). Does usually get a CDT booster 4-6 weeks before kidding. Children receive a course of CDT immunizations at 5, 8, 12, and occasionally 16 weeks of age.

Regular deworming and other preventative medical care will also be necessary for the doe and her offspring. Deworm children start at 6–8 weeks of age. One or two weeks after the doe has kidded, deworm her, and collaborate with your veterinarian to create a deworming schedule for the adult animals in your community. Sometimes external parasites are a problem, so be sure to frequently examine your pet's skin and hair for any irritation or problems.

The hooves of goats will require occasional clipping (at least once a year and possibly more frequently). Goats' hair must also be trimmed in preparation for displays.

Before adding a freshly acquired goat to your herd, keep it segregated from the other animals for at least 30 days. To stop the infection from spreading to your other animals, it's critical to keep a watchful eye out for any illnesses or other potential problems with the new addition.

Managing Milk

You will need to breed your does once a year. Before being bred, does should be eight months old or, if they are not little breeds, at least 80 pounds. Doe breeding usually occurs in the fall. Does ovulate every eighteen to twenty-one days for three days. Maintain a distance between your bucks and does until they become fertile. After breeding, they ought to be split up once more to avoid an odd taste in the milk.

Giving birth, or kidding, usually occurs 150 days after breeding. has triplets occasionally and twins most of the time. The doe will freshen, or start to make milk, after giving birth. She can continue to lactate for up to ten months if she is constantly milked.

After a run of milk production, does ought to be given a minimum of two months to dehydrate completely before engaging in further breeding.

Goats yield so much milk that you may let the young ones nurse and yet consume the excess. After the goats are two weeks old, most goat farmers cage the young ones overnight and milk them in the morning. The kids can breastfeed whenever they choose to after the morning milking.

How to Milk a Goat for the First Time

It's not too difficult to milk a goat, especially if you have hands-on instruction from an experienced farmer. During the milking season, many feed grain to the does. Maintaining a regular milking time is crucial. You will milk once or twice a day, spaced around twelve hours apart. Naturally, you must ensure that the location and tools you use for milking the goat are clean and that you may immediately cool the milk after milking it.

It makes sense that a goat might feel a bit anxious when she gives birth and freshens for the first time because she is surrounded by unfamiliar objects and situations. She might reply with outright rejection the first time she's ready to be milked. Trying to fight her will simply make her more determined to resist, and it can even end up hurting you or her. Therefore, while you are milking a novice, it is best to have a powerful partner beside you.

I urge you to prepare your milking area in advance and leave space for a milking stand equipped with a stanchion for her safe and secure holding. This is a safe method and will eventually become a pleasant spot for her to be milked.

As she places the feed in front of her in the stanchion, have your assistant tightly grasp her rear legs to prevent her from moving. Regardless of what occurs once you begin milking, simply continue until the task is completed. She might kick, stamp, shout, lunge, or lie down. Simply continue milking as steadily and rhythmically as you can. Talk to her gently and reassuringly; occasionally, I sing while milking. You're fostering safety and trust by treating her justly and firmly. Make sure to show her some affection as a treat.

Until she understands that being milked doesn't endanger her safety and that resistance is ineffective, you'll probably need to repeat this practice multiple times for a few days, if not a week or longer.

9 | Meat, Fiber, and Other Products

Raising Goats for Meat Production

Many people profit from selling "meat goats" or "market goats," which are goats raised specifically to sell their meat as opposed to goats raised for other reasons, such as dairy production or pet ownership.

The demand for goat meat in the US is growing significantly, which means that producing meat goats has good profit potential. Goat meat's superior health benefits over other meats are a plus. It has roughly 3/4 of the calories in chicken and about 2/3 of the calories in beef. Moreover, its fat content is 1/3 that of pig and less than half that of chicken.

Goat meat is in such high demand that the majority of it is imported from nations outside the United States, such as Australia. For this reason, it's possible to make money from growing meat goats. There are a few things you must accomplish before you can begin raising meat goats.

Be cautious about who you purchase meat goats from when you first start doing it. Make a ton of inquiries. Goat breeders occasionally sell goats because something is wrong with them, and you don't want their issues to become your problems.

This may seem simple, but when it comes to meat goats in particular, you want to search for goats that will thrive outside with little care, have a high meat content, and have a good probability of giving birth to several kids on their own with little help.

Generally speaking, there should be one buck for every thirty to fifty does. Although mixed-breed does are OK, aim for a full-bred buck.

Since a high-quality buck will be breeding with numerous does and extending his line across your herd that might last you for many years, concentrate on spending a little bit extra for him. Try to save money by using a cheap buck, and you can end up with long-term difficulties.

When evaluating a goat's suitability for producing meat, seek out those that appear robust, robust, heavy, and healthy—rather than obese and gaunt.

When viewed from the front or side, a goat's body should appear balanced, and its back should be level and straight. The goat's body should have a huge barrel, but not a potbelly. The rumen of the goat, which breaks down the feed, needs a lot of space.

Long, wide, and deep loins translate into more flesh for the goat from the ribs to the rump.

Selecting does mean selecting people who are not too elderly but who have already had at least one child. Since they have already shown to be fertile, you want those who have already given birth.

Inquire with the seller about any challenges or problems the doe has had when kidding. As soon as your herd is established with a few goats, you must prepare to care for them.

Feeding Market or Meat Goats

The obvious objective with meat goats is to increase their muscle mass, as this will increase their meat production.

You should provide them with access to forages, grains, minerals, and water, just like you would with other goats.

However, you also need to feed the market goat protein supplements. You must add these supplements to the grain you feed your meat goats to raise the grain's protein content to between 14% and 18%.

The more aggressive goats may steal food from the less aggressive goats if you feed a large number of goats grain at once. By giving each goat the equivalent of roughly 2 pounds of feed each feeding, you may prevent that issue and ensure that each goat receives an equal portion.

For your goats' diet to be free of digestive problems, the feed must contain at least 18% fiber. All of this is presuming that you are providing them with pasture, hay, or fodder regularly.

For market goats, you might want to think about using cow feed rather than goat or horse feed, which can be more expensive for the same effects.

Feeding your meat goats is a significant expense. It can mean the difference between a herd that is profitable for you and one that is unsustainable and costs you money. Profitable meat goat farmers frequently come up with inventive solutions to reduce feeding expenses.

It is best if you have a large amount of land where the goats can have access to natural forage.

Some people who don't have a lot of land arrange for their goats to graze on forested areas that belong to someone else, such as regions that require brush clearing or federal grounds that can be open to free grazing.

Some make deals with brewers to receive their wet spent grain—which is still suitable for use as goat feed—for free. Your herd will be more lucrative the more you can utilize free or readily available grain or forage sources outside of it.

Marketing Meat Goats

If you are raising meat goats, you can market them by selling them through various channels, based on whatever is most economical for you at the moment. Some producers of meat goats choose to sell their product to an auction house or trader to save time, but doing so will force you to accept a lower price.

Some farms might choose to sell straight to a restaurant, meat processor, or even a customer purchasing for their use, cutting out the intermediary. Everything relies on the best deals you can negotiate.

Demand for Goat Skins and Fiber

Goat Skins

Goat skins can also be used to make money. If you labor carefully to remove skins with as little damage as possible, you can make more money if you slaughter and process goats yourself for meat.

To keep the skin from drying out, becoming infected, or becoming damaged, you will need to understand how to care for it once it has been removed. More expensive skins will cost more money.

Goat skins are perfect for leatherworking, African drum manufacturing, and other crafts, and there are many individuals interested in purchasing them.

Compared to cow leather, goat leather is thought to be softer and more resilient. Goat skins can be purchased for as little as $15 or as much as $65 on eBay, depending on the color and quality of the skin.

That might not seem like a lot of cash. But remember, this is just one of many revenue streams that your goat herd can produce, and they all add up.

Besides, you will be de-skinning the goats if you process your meat. When you can sell them, why throw them away?

Goat Fiber (Hair)

Using the fiber (hair) from slaughtered goats, you can diversify your revenue sources even more. Goats breed for mohair or angora.

Cashmere can be produced by other goats. To be clear, the fiber is not the typical hair found in a goat's outer coat; rather, it is the softer substance (similar to fuzz) that comes from the undercoat.

With the high demand and high cost of both mohair and cashmere, this kind of goat business has profit potential. You can generate fiber from your goats while you are rearing them for slaughter in the future, as fiber is often combed or cut from live goats.

You can charge a pound for the fiber, but if you additionally handle cleaning, preparing it for spinning, or making yarn out of it before you sell it, you can make a little extra money.

In these circumstances, you can get a lot more money per pound for it. Additionally, a lot of goat farmers harvest fiber from dairy goats. You will most likely need a large herd to accomplish this because it takes a lot of fiber to produce an amount large enough to sell.

Financial Considerations

You must take the time to create a thorough financial business plan that includes estimates of year-over-year income, expenses, investment needed, borrowing needed, and cash flow timing if you want to succeed financially with market goats.

However, there are additional financial factors that distinguish successful meat-goat enterprises from unsuccessful ones.

History demonstrates that trying to start too big and grow too fast is one of the main mistakes made by breeders entering the meat goat industry for the first time.

It's preferable to start small and expand gradually as you become more knowledgeable and successful.

In light of this, if your goal is to become a successful meat goat breeder, concentrate on establishing connections with more seasoned breeders who can offer reliable guidance throughout the process.

Additionally, control your financial expectations and hold off on expecting your herd to turn a large profit too soon. Consider it a gradual investment in your ability to raise meat goats in the future.

Establishing a superior meat goat herd requires persistence and patience. Arranging dependable long-term funding also helps you weather the ups and downs of your gradual growth.

This lessens the possibility of financial strain forcing you to take on too much too quickly.

Starting with a portion of the business that will give you some early experience and allow you to start small until you learn more about market goats is a fantastic way to ease into the financial requirements of a meat goat business.

You may choose goats, for instance, breed them, and then sell the offspring to other breeders for use as brood stock. This will introduce you to the process of choosing, breeding, growing, and selling meat goats while requiring less capital than a sizable market goat herd.

For a lesser financial outlay, you can also try your hand at exhibiting your goats in meat goat events. This is an excellent opportunity to network with other breeders, gain some insight into the industry, and become knowledgeable about various meat goat varieties.

Recall to be patient, take advice from reliable sources, develop gradually, and make thorough plans. You won't get wealthy overnight if you follow my advice, but your market goat business will gradually grow into a thriving enterprise.

CONCLUSION

Goats may improve our lives in so many ways, from playing children in the field to the warm mug of fresh milk in your hand. From selecting the ideal breed to taking care of their health and enjoying their bountiful harvest, raising these lively animals has given you the knowledge and self-assurance to go out on a fulfilling trip.

Recall that caring for goats is a relationship rather than just a task. It's about observing their curious gaze, hearing their bleats, and comprehending their amusing personalities. It's about providing a safe place for them to flourish in, and then reaping the rewards of your labor by eating fleece, cheese, and meat.

Remember this as you manage the pleasures and difficulties of owning a goat: in addition to providing care for animals, you are also developing a relationship with nature, supporting a sustainable way of life, and improving your own life via the wonder and friendship these amazing animals bring.

So accept the bleating chorus, the muddy hooves, and the never-ending entertainment. I hope your trip with goats is full of joy, education, and the constant fulfillment that comes from living a life enriched by these fascinating animals. With the knowledge you now possess, you are well on your way to building a rewarding relationship with your own herd. After all, the happiest goats live with the happiest owners.